WEATHER OPERATIONS

Air Force Doctrine Document 3-59
3 May 2006

Incorporating Change 1, 28 July 2011

This document complements related discussion found in Joint Publication 3-59, *Meteorological and Oceanographic Operations*.

Cover Sheet for Air Force Doctrine Document (AFDD) 3-59, *Weather Operations*

OPR: LeMay Center/DD

28 July 2011

AFDD numbering has changed to correspond with the joint doctrine publication numbering architecture (the AFDD titles remain unchanged until the doctrine is revised). Any AFDD citations within the documents will list the old AFDD numbers until the doctrine is revised. The changed numbers follow:

OLD	NEW	TITLE
AFDD 2-1	changed to AFDD 3-1	*Air Warfare*
AFDD 2-1.1	changed to AFDD 3-01	*Counterair Operations*
AFDD 2-1.2	changed to AFDD 3-70	*Strategic Attack*
AFDD 2-1.3	changed to AFDD 3-03	*Counterland Operations*
AFDD 2-1.4	changed to AFDD 3-04	*Countersea Operations*
AFDD 2-1.6	changed to AFDD 3-50	*Personnel Recovery Operations*
AFDD 2-1.7	changed to AFDD 3-52	*Airspace Control*
AFDD 2-1.8	changed to AFDD 3-40	*Counter-CBRN*
AFDD 2-1.9	changed to AFDD 3-60	*Targeting*
AFDD 2-10	changed to AFDD 3-27	*Homeland Operations*
AFDD 2-12	changed to AFDD 3-72	*Nuclear Operations*
AFDD 2-2	changed to AFDD 3-14	*Space Operations*
AFDD 2-2.1	changed to AFDD 3-14.1	*Counterspace Operations*
AFDD 2-3	changed to AFDD 3-24	*Irregular Warfare*
AFDD 2-3.1	changed to AFDD 3-22	*Foreign Internal Defense*
AFDD 2-4	changed to AFDD 4-0	*Combat Support*
AFDD 2-4.1	changed to AFDD 3-10	*Force Protection*
AFDD 2-4.2	changed to AFDD 4-02	*Health Services*
AFDD 2-4.4	changed to AFDD 4-11	*Bases, Infrastructure, and Facilities* [Rescinded]
AFDD 2-4.5	changed to AFDD 1-04	*Legal Support*
AFDD 2-5	changed to AFDD 3-13	*Information Operations*
AFDD 2-5.1	changed to AFDD 3-13.1	*Electronic Warfare*
AFDD 2-5.3	changed to AFDD 3-61	*Public Affairs Operations*
AFDD 2-6	changed to AFDD 3-17	*Air Mobility Operations*
AFDD 2-7	changed to AFDD 3-05	*Special Operations*
AFDD 2-8	changed to AFDD 6-0	*Command and Control*
AFDD 2-9	changed to AFDD 2-0	*ISR Operations*
AFDD 2-9.1	changed to AFDD 3-59	*Weather Operations*

BY ORDER OF THE
SECRETARY OF THE AIR FORCE

AIR FORCE DOCTRINE DOCUMENT 3-59
3 MAY 2006
INCORPORATING CHANGE 1, 28 JULY 2011 |

SUMMARY OF CHANGES

This Interim change to Air Force Doctrine Document (AFDD) 2-9.1 changes the cover to AFDD 3-59, *Weather Operations* to reflect revised AFI 10-1301, Air Force Doctrine (9 August 2010). AFDD numbering has changed to correspond with the joint doctrine publication numbering architecture. AFDD titles and content remain unchanged until updated in the next full revision. A margin bar indicates newly revised material.

OPR: LeMay Center/DD
Certified by: LeMay Center/DD (Col Todd C. Westhauser)
Pages: 42
Accessibility: Available on the e-publishing website at www.e-publishing.af.mil for
                downloading
Releasability: There are no releasability restrictions on this publication
Approved by: LeMay Center/CC, Maj Gen Thomas K. Andersen, USAF
            Commander, LeMay Center for Doctrine Development and Education

FOREWORD

The Department of Defense operates in a challenging natural environment stretching from the surface of the earth into the far reaches of space. While the environment has beleaguered military operations for centuries, it has also provided strategic, operational, and tactical advantage to the forewarned. Sun Tzu once proclaimed, "Know the ground, know the weather; your victory will be total." Indeed, history has shown that commanders who have exploited knowledge of the environment and its effects have been rewarded with victory, while those who have ignored the environment have often met with failure.

Air Force weather operations are now more sophisticated, accurate, and precise than ever, presenting air, space, and surface forces with an even greater opportunity to exploit knowledge of the natural environment as a force multiplier. This can only be accomplished, however, when commanders integrate environmental information and its effects on operations into all aspects of planning, execution, assessment and sustainment. It is an essential element on the road to victory.

JAMES F. JACKSON
Brigadier General, USAF
Commander

TABLE OF CONTENTS

INTRODUCTION

PURPOSE

This Air Force doctrine document (AFDD) establishes doctrinal guidance for organizing weather forces and employing weather operations capabilities in support of air, space, and surface forces at the operational level of conflict. It is a critical element of Air Force operational-level doctrine and as such should form the basis from which Air Force and Army commanders integrate weather capabilities into their operations. Air Force tactics, techniques, and procedures should complement this doctrine at the tactical level.

APPLICATION

This AFDD applies to the Total Force: all Air Force military and civilian personnel, including regular, Air Force Reserve Command, and Air National Guard units and members.

Unless specifically stated otherwise, Air Force doctrine applies to the full range of military operations, as appropriate, from stability, security, transition, and reconstruction operations to major combat operations.

The doctrine in this document is authoritative, but not directive. Therefore, commanders need to consider the contents of this AFDD and the particular situation when accomplishing their missions. Airmen should read it, discuss it, and practice it.

SCOPE

This doctrine for Air Force weather operations provides a firm foundation for integrating weather capabilities into the planning, execution, assessment, and sustainment of Air Force and Army air, space, and surface operations. A common doctrine helps ensure weather organizations at all echelons provide commanders and forces with timely, accurate, and relevant environmental information and that commanders and their forces exploit this information smartly. Since weather operations complement intelligence, surveillance, and reconnaissance (ISR) operations in the development of battlespace awareness, this document has been made a subordinate publication of AFDD 2-9, *Intelligence, Surveillance, and Reconnaissance Operations.*

COMAFFOR / JFACC / CFACC
A note on terminology

One of the cornerstones of Air Force doctrine is that "the US Air Force prefers - and in fact, plans and trains - to employ through a commander, Air Force forces (COMAFFOR), who is also dual-hatted as a joint force air and space component commander (JFACC)." (AFDD 1)

To simplify the use of nomenclature, Air Force doctrine documents will assume the COMAFFOR is dual-hatted as the JFACC unless specifically stated otherwise. The term "COMAFFOR" refers to the Air Force Service component commander while the term "JFACC" refers to the joint component-level operational commander.

While both joint and Air Force doctrine state that one individual will normally be dual-hatted as COMAFFOR and JFACC, the two responsibilities are different, and should be executed through different staffs.

Normally, the COMAFFOR function executes operational control/administrative control of assigned and attached Air Force forces through a Service A-staff while the JFACC function executes tactical control of joint air and space component forces through an air and space operations center (AOC).

When multinational operations are involved, the JFACC becomes a combined force air and space component commander (CFACC). Likewise, the air and space operations center, though commonly referred to as an AOC, in joint or combined operations is correctly known as a JAOC or CAOC.

FOUNDATIONAL DOCTRINE STATEMENTS

Foundational doctrine statements are the basic principles and beliefs upon which Air Force doctrine documents (AFDDs) are built. Other information in the AFDD expands on or supports these statements.

✪ Air Force weather operations are critical to a commander's battlespace awareness across the range of military operations. (Page 1)

✪ Air Force weather operations predict when the natural environment will affect friendly and enemy air, space, and surface operations—a key ingredient of predictive battlespace awareness—possibly offering friendly force commanders an exploitable asymmetrical advantage. (Page 1)

✪ Air Force and joint weather operations should provide combat forces at all echelons with consistent information, resulting in "one operation, one forecast." (Page 6)

✪ Air Force weather forces execute five core processes—collection, analysis, prediction, tailoring, and integration—to characterize the environment and exploit environmental information. (Page 8)

✪ Prior to military operations, Air Force and joint/coalition weather forces should develop a strategy to maximize the effectiveness of environmental data collection efforts in theater to satisfy strategic, operational, and tactical requirements. (Page 10)

✪ Air Force weather operations with global, regional, and local scopes provide direct support to strategic, operational, and tactical decision-makers through a combination of reachback and distributed operations (e.g., on-site). (Page 16)

✪ Reachback and distributed operations provide the ability to reliably access environmental information and resources while minimizing the theater footprint. (Page 19)

✪ Air Force weather capabilities should be integrated with those of other Services and nations to provide coherent and structured weather operations to joint and multinational forces. (Page 21)

✪ Air Force weather operations employ Airmen educated in the sciences of meteorology and space physics, trained to couple this science with the art of military operations, and capable of operating in permissive, uncertain, and hostile environments. (Page 27)

CHAPTER ONE

OVERVIEW OF WEATHER OPERATIONS

In military operations, weather is the first step in planning and the final determining factor in the execution of any mission.

—General Carl "Tooey" Spaatz
First Chief of Staff of the Air Force (CSAF)

GENERAL

Air Force weather operations are an operational function of air and space power (Air Force Doctrine Document [AFDD] 1, *Air Force Basic Doctrine*). They provide direct support to conventional and special operations forces (SOF) of the Air Force and, by an inter-Service support agreement based on the National Security Act of 1947, the US Army. When designated, Air Force weather forces also provide direct support to joint, coalition, and other agency operations.

Air Force weather operations are critical to a commander's battlespace awareness across the range of military operations. Few military endeavors, including those of our adversaries, are immune to the effects of the environment. Neglected or ignored, the weather and its effects can doom even the most carefully planned and executed campaigns and operations. Properly applied, Air Force weather operations can provide our air, space, and surface forces with a significant, even decisive, advantage over our enemies.

Air Force weather operations predict when the natural environment will affect friendly and enemy air, space, and surface operations—a key ingredient of predictive battlespace awareness (PBA)—possibly offering friendly force commanders an exploitable asymmetrical advantage. Air Force weather operators are globally vigilant, persistently monitoring, assessing, and reporting the state of the natural environment. To be relevant to decision-makers, Air Force weather forces should know the past, current and future state of the atmosphere and space environment and then translate that into impacts on operations. In essence, weather operations provide two distinct yet related basic functions: 1) describing past, current, and future environmental conditions, and 2) enabling the exploitation of environmental information at key decision points.

Battlefield commanders need past, current and future weather information, a truth inherent in war since ancient times. As such, the second basic function of weather operations most directly impacts military operations. In this aspect, weather forces enable the exploitation of actionable environmental information at key decision points during all phases of military operations. Furthermore, weather information is ideal if linked with intelligence, surveillance, and reconnaissance (ISR) information to enable battlespace awareness from the strategic to tactical levels of warfare. Commanders at all levels should use environmental information to optimize Air Force and Army capabilities as force providers to the joint force and functional component commanders.

The Range of Air Force Weather Operations

Traditionally, the term 'weather' has referred to the state of the atmosphere (with respect to temperature, precipitation, sky condition, visibility, etc.). From the earliest days of aviation, a great deal of effort has been focused on developing "all weather" aircraft and weapons. However, as technological advances have allowed us to overcome the constraints of basic sensible weather effects, this same technology has fallen prey to the effects of other, often invisible environmental impacts. For example, precision navigation using GPS technology can still be adversely affected by solar flares and electromagnetic disturbances undetectable by human senses. Weather, or the broader term "environmental information," increasingly encompasses a full spectrum of visible, sensible, and electromagnetic natural phenomena and conditions affecting operations in and through the terrestrial and space environments.

—Various Sources

Weather effects should be integral to the planning, execution, and sustainment of any operation. Commanders should consider and account for weather and space environmental effects on operations during development and design of deliberate and contingency plans, consistent with the joint force commander's (JFC's) strategy and objectives. Operationally relevant climatology based on clearly defined environmental effects criteria greatly assists in:

☼ Preparing strategies and courses of action (COAs).

☼ Identifying opportunities to exploit environmental conditions for military advantage.

☼ Assessing feasibility of certain types of air, space, and surface missions.

☼ Anticipating effectiveness of platforms/weapons systems and munitions.

☼ Determining optimal seasons, times, and locations for conducting operations.

☼ Evaluating logistical, survivability (health/safety), and quality-of-life requirements.

Air Force weather operations are also a key element of non-combat military activities such as stability operations and relief efforts. Virtually all forces that conduct or support these types of operations are influenced by the weather. Weather and space environmental effects on operations should therefore be considered in every facet of planning, deployment, employment, and redeployment.

Commanders and planners should consider the implications of executing air, space, and surface operations during particular seasons to maximize effectiveness and ensure success. In Operation ENDURING FREEDOM, commanders preferred to conduct operations in mountainous Afghanistan before the onset of the typically harsh winter, an environment more advantageous to the home-based adversary.

Conversely, during Operation IRAQI FREEDOM, they opted to initiate combat in Iraq prior to the 100-plus degree summer that would have drastically reduced the capabilities of US forces wearing mission-oriented protective posture gear. Commanders should integrate environmental factors early in the planning process to ensure all effects on operations are considered.

—Various Sources

To optimize employment of friendly force capabilities, Air Force weather forces support research, development, acquisition, and testing of Air Force and Army weapons and weapons systems, identifying and documenting environmental sensitivities. System designers can then attempt to mitigate these sensitivities through appropriate system modifications; Air Force weather forces can forecast impacts based on these sensitivities, allowing commanders to mitigate the effects through modifications to the mission profile. To highlight opportunities to exploit asymmetric environmental effects on enemy capabilities, weather forces work with the intelligence community to identify and document the weather sensitivities of threat forces and systems. Weather and space environmental information should also be integrated into simulations, exercises, and war games in order to capture the environmental effects on operations, training, and acquisition. Properly portraying weather in modeling and simulation (M&S) activities addresses the Secretary of Defense's mandate to "train as we fight." The requirement for the Air Force's emerging distributed mission operations program to provide immersive mission rehearsal environments is better satisfied with realistically modeled weather. Furthermore, including weather in M&S ensures weather effects on operations are accounted for in planning scenarios, results of virtual weapons tests are more representative, and strategy and tactics learned in war games are more realistic.

PRINCIPLES OF WEATHER OPERATIONS

Air Force weather operations are fruitless if environmental information is not properly exploited by friendly force commanders. Exploitation can only occur when planners and decision-makers understand weather and space effects on operations and use this knowledge in a timely manner. For instance, aircrews can exploit cloud cover and precipitation to conceal friendly movement from enemy aircraft or ground observation. Properly integrated into the decision-making process, air and space weather forecasts can be used to enhance friendly offensive and defensive operations and, at the same time, identify those occasions when the enemy cannot exploit the natural environment for sanctuary.

Air Force weather forces are driven by four timeless principles: accuracy, relevancy, timeliness, and consistency.

Accuracy

Air Force weather operations must provide accurate environmental information to decision-makers, a continual challenge for scientists and weather operators. Limited measurement coverage and shortfalls in forecast technology reduce accuracy, but weather forces strive to overcome these impediments.

The warfighter actively contributes to accuracy by relaying the latest mission-area environmental conditions to weather forces. Observations from manual and automated pilot reports (PIREPS) and observations from the first wave of aircraft launched prior to the main force package, for example, allow weather personnel to improve the accuracy of weather effects on follow-on missions. Post-strike in-flight reports should include target area and other relevant weather information.

Relevancy

Environmental information must be relevant to air, space, and surface operations. Air Force weather forces should ensure commanders receive information on weather parameters that have the potential to degrade or enhance any mission. Commanders, in turn, should assess the expected performance of their assets in light of weather and space impacts to determine the proper combination of delivery systems, munitions, platforms, and other resources to attain desired effects.

Air Force weather operations are most relevant when integrated into the operational planning process. Environmental information should directly apply to planning, conducting, assessing, and sustaining operations. Air Force weather operations focus on the joint force and component commanders' operational requirements, known or planned courses of action, specific planned and executable missions, and commander's objectives. Joint operations can be more successful when commanders are given an opportunity to plan for operationally relevant weather conditions.

Linebacker I, 1972

North Vietnamese forces conducted an unexpected offensive into South Vietnam in early 1972 despite Seventh Air Force bombing operations in the invasion zone. Meticulously exploiting low cloud ceilings and visibility during the transition between monsoons, the North Vietnamese were able to move an entire division of 160 tanks across the DMZ without much detection or resistance from the air.

Only one out of the first twelve days of the invasion provided sufficient weather for American aircraft to effectively attack division targets. Seventh Air Force leadership soon learned the value of integrating operationally relevant weather information into their decision cycles. Forecast weather conditions across the theater became a vital consideration in planning Linebacker I missions. Target selections for the next 24 hours were made based on weather forecasts. Weapons systems were configured and munitions chosen based on performance in specific types of weather. Frag orders for the next 3-4 days were built using long-range weather forecasts.

—John F. Fuller,
Thor's Legions: Weather Support to the
U.S. Air Force and Army, 1937-1987

Air Force weather forces should cultivate a two-way flow of information in which operators provide relevant mission data that can be used to enhance the relevancy of environmental information to operations. Weather personnel should understand the strengths, limitations, and time factors associated with specific air and space systems and land missions and fine-tune environmental data accordingly based on the specific situation. For instance, weather that could negatively affect air refueling operations, such as excessive turbulence and cloud cover in the 18,000 to 24,000-foot flight level range, will not be relevant to Army helicopters operating below 500 feet. Without a detailed understanding of operations and mission profiles, environmental information runs the risk of being irrelevant.

Timeliness

Environmental information should be provided in time to influence the decision-making process and to plan and execute operations. Environmental information should be the latest available, and it should be quickly disseminated and integrated at the appropriate time into operations. Weather personnel should also be vigilant and responsive, informing commanders of potential environmental effects on proposed air, space, and surface operations in a timely manner. Air Force weather operations, therefore, rely heavily on assured communications to realize the principle of timeliness.

THE 3RD SCOUTING FORCE, USAAF, 8TH AIR FORCE

Originally constituted as the 3rd Air Division Scouting Force in August 1944, this force consisted of eight volunteer pilots with command or lead pilot experience and at least one tour of operations on B-17 or B-24 bombers. All pilots received weather observation training and a 20-hour conversion course on the P-51 Mustang before posting to Station 159 at Wormingford, England.

Their primary task in September 1944 was to fly P-51 fighters to scout target visibility ahead of the 3rd Air Division bombers. With their designated task of reporting meteorological conditions, it was a logical step to expand this capability by using the services of a professional meteorologist. In January 1945, 1st Lt. Ivan D. Carlton (meteorologist) was tasked with reorganizing and expanding the operational role of the unit. In addition to the P-51 target scouts, eight B-17s arrived on the scene, stripped of most of their defensive armament for increased cruising speed. The B-17s were crewed by a pilot, co-pilot, navigator, engineer, radio operator, tail gunner and a meteorologist. The B-17s scouted the weather throughout the European Theatre of Operations.

The unit inherited the table of organization from the 862nd Bomb Squadron on 1 February 1945 and became the 3rd Scouting and Weather Force. By the war's end they had flown 132 missions, completing 1,300 individual sorties.

—Various Sources

A significant aspect of timeliness is how environmental information is disseminated to the warfighter. Machine-to-machine dissemination improves the chances that critical weather information and its impact on operations will reach decision-makers in time to capitalize on time-sensitive opportunities and other operations. For instance, real-time information to the cockpit (such as images of targets as affected by the weather and accounting for sensor wavelengths) enhances situational awareness for newly received time-sensitive targets. Similarly, space situational awareness (SSA) requires timely integration of accurate and relevant environmental data into military space operations. Being able to distinguish between enemy jammers and natural sources of interference on our space systems enables the commander of joint space operations (JSO) to identify threat trends to better protect our space center of gravity.

Consistency

Air Force and joint weather operations should provide combat forces at all echelons with consistent information regarding the state of the natural environment, resulting in "one operation, one forecast." Weather forces produce, access, and incorporate the same basic set of data in developing assessments of weather effects to operations, ensuring similar results. Natural environmental information provided to commanders across the levels of conflict should therefore be spatially and temporally consistent across the theater, operation, and/or battlespace, as appropriate.

CHAPTER TWO

THE WEATHER OPERATIONS PROCESS

> *Weather, of course, remains the final factor in the decision where each day or night's activities shall be employed, and that puts a very great responsibility in the hands of the officers who actually handle these great, enormous masses of aircraft.*
>
> —Winston S. Churchill

GENERAL

Air Force weather operations execute five core processes—collection, analysis, prediction, tailoring, and integration—to characterize the environment and exploit environmental information. These processes should be routinely evaluated to ensure environmental information is timely, accurate, relevant, and

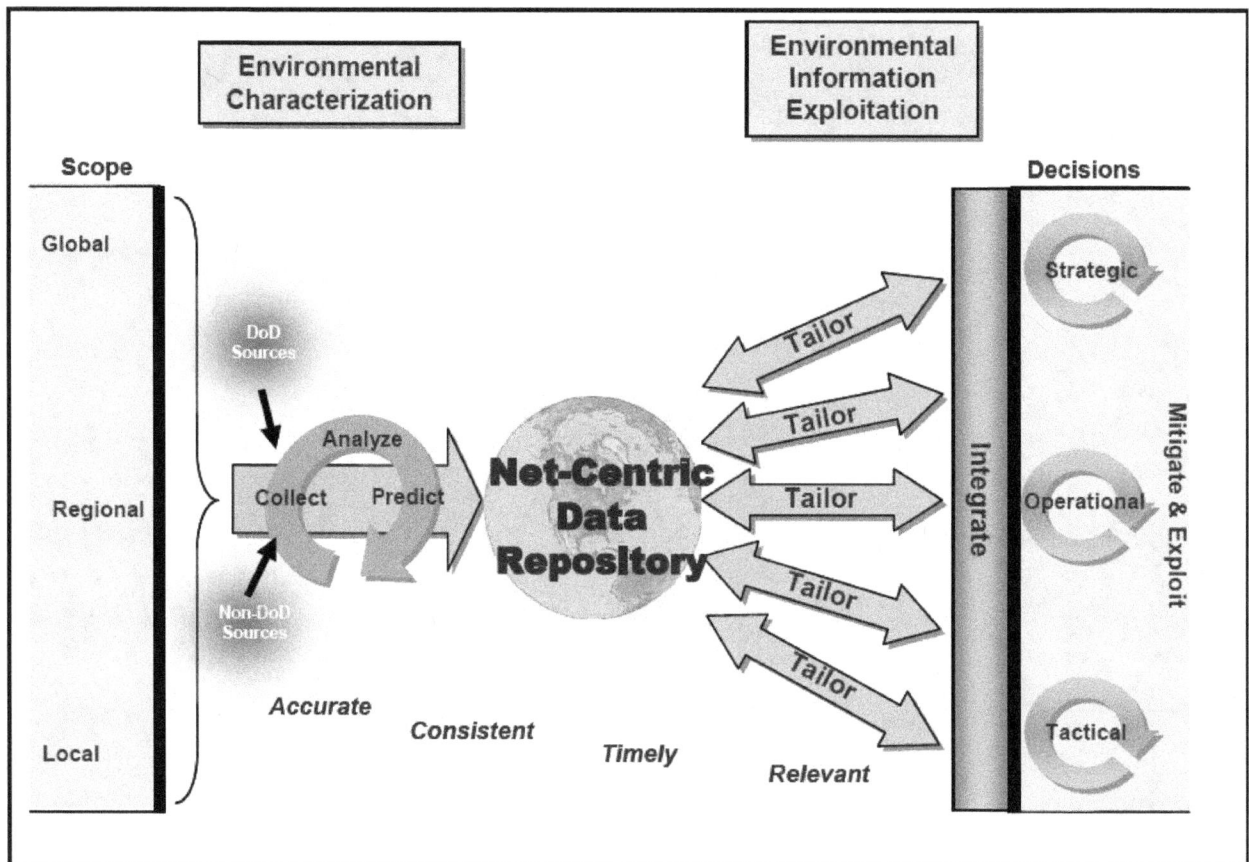

Figure 2.1 Conceptual Model of Air Force Weather Operations

consistent. Effective evaluation quantifies the quality of the weather data and environmental impact information provided, which is critical to decision-makers' confidence. It also detects deficiencies and helps focus corrective actions where needed most.

COLLECT

The weather operations process depends on the collection of high-quality data that sets the foundation for enhancing operational missions. Collection is the essential component of worldwide and regional databases from which weather products are derived.

> **The Weather Operations Process:**
>
> *Collect*
> *Analyze*
> *Predict*
> *Tailor*
> *Integrate*

Air Force weather forces collect terrestrial and space environmental information from across the globe. These data include weather and space observations, meteorological satellite (METSAT) data, and weather radar imagery from worldwide military, civilian, and commercial sources. Since each collection capability has limitations, Air Force weather operations seek an optimal blend of measurements from ground-, sea-, air-, and space-based sensors. Although the Department of Defense (DOD) owns some of these sensors, such as those flown on the Defense Meteorological Satellite Program constellation, most international data are gathered via data-sharing agreements between the US and other countries. While foreign data greatly improve the coverage of measurements across the globe, the DOD retains an assured global weather collection capability. A continual collection of weather and space data contributes to accuracy of products.

The Critical View from Space

Commercial and military METSAT imagery, from both geostationary and polar orbiting platforms, is the centerpiece of environmental data collection. Defense Meteorological Satellite Program platforms, for instance, provide secure high-resolution imagery that is used to identify mission-limiting weather. Effective downlink and data-sharing solutions improve weather operations by ensuring imagery and data are delivered with minimal delay to widely dispersed users.

—Various Sources

Insufficient sources or availability of environmental data may exist in regions where air, space, and surface operations occur. Air Force weather forces therefore maintain a capability to deploy in-theater, in close coordination with joint and coalition weather forces, to establish an environmental data collection network in support of the full range of air, space, and surface operations. In addition, non-traditional weather data sources—such as ISR platforms and sensors and unmanned aerial vehicles—significantly enhance the quality and quantity of theater environmental data collection, especially in data-sparse areas. Commanders should emphasize these non-traditional weather collection efforts throughout an operation and ensure Air Force weather forces receive these data in a timely manner. Such data may provide the only, or possibly the critical, piece of environmental information pivotal to mission success. Complete and accurate weather observations are a vital aid in the development of a meteorological history and trends for new operational areas.

PIREPS hit the mark in Cambodia, 1974-75

US Air Force C-130 aircrews conducting aerial resupply missions over Cambodia in late 1973 found that just 70-85 percent of vital ammunition and food bundles landed in their intended drop zones. Those that went awry often ended up in communist Khmer Rouge hands. Since the aircraft were dropping from over 13,000 feet to minimize enemy air defense threats, upper-level winds in and near the drop zones were often the culprit. Weather operations personnel had difficulty producing accurate forecasts of winds between drop altitude and the surface due to a shortage of upper air weather observations from within Cambodia. A renewed call for PIREPS from C-130 aircrews reaped lasting dividends. Forecasters collected valuable information on wind speed and direction over the region from the crews and rapidly incorporated this (otherwise unobtainable) data into weather briefings for upcoming missions. By late 1974 the improved wind forecasts enabled nearly 99 per cent of all bundles dropped in country to land in their targeted areas, where needy Cambodians defending their homeland were able to recover them. In particular, 196 additional bundles worth over $1.1million arrived at Kompong Selia between August 1974 and January 1975.

—**John F. Fuller,** *Weather and War*

Prior to military operations, Air Force and joint/coalition weather forces should develop a strategy to maximize the effectiveness of environmental data collection efforts in theater to satisfy strategic, operational, and tactical requirements. This is critically important to achieving weather information dominance in the battlespace. The collection strategy should identify all sources of weather and space observations for integration into theater and global databases. It should also leverage weather sensor packages deployed on manned and unmanned platforms, weather sensors deployed across the battlespace, and robust communication architectures (to reduce delay of environmental information transmission). The environmental collection plan to exploit non-traditional sensors/platforms should be integrated into the overall ISR theater sensing strategy to enhance battlespace awareness.

Meteorologists regarded the airplane as yet another capability for observing the weather. Special aircraft were initially sent out to record visibility information from above. By the late 1920s instruments for measuring pressure, aircraft temperature, and humidity were attached to the external surfaces of aircraft such as the DeHavilland DH-4.

The development of specialized meteorological equipment in the mid-1930s brought an end to the days of the aircraft as an intentional means for obtaining upper-air weather observations during peacetime.

—**John F. Fuller**
Thor's Legions: Weather Support to the U.S. Air Force and Army, 1937-1987

ANALYZE

Analysis entails building a coherent, integrated depiction of the past and current state of the natural environment over a specified region. An effective analysis of collected weather data helps ensure the accuracy of forecast information provided to commanders. It enables identification of environmental features and conditions—important to air, space, and surface operations—requiring subsequent study and monitoring. Further analysis determines strength, movement, and timing of these features and their mission-impacting elements (such as temperature, cloud cover, and ionospheric scintillation) based on critical weather threshold sensitivities. These analyzed data are processed and assimilated into environmental databases to provide battlespace awareness and inputs for decision-making and predictions.

Analysis determines strength, movement, and timing of environmental features and their mission-impacting elements

PREDICT

Air Force weather operations use collected and analyzed data to predict future environmental conditions and their impacts on operations. Forecasts are only as sound as their initial inputs. Accurate forecasts therefore depend upon robust collection and meticulous analysis of environmental data.

Forecasting is a synergistic process between man and machine. Highly trained, experienced weather personnel refine computer model output to produce detailed forecasts, which include temporal and spatial assessments of terrestrial and space weather features and associated environmental elements. For this process to continually improve, it is important that feedback from actual conditions be received to improve the forecasting models.

TAILOR

Environmental information must be tailored to the unique air, space, and surface operational requirements of the joint force. Weather and space products should be custom-built based on known, specific environmental sensitivities and effects to operations and systems. For example, decision aids, weather effects matrices (i.e., stoplight charts), and target-area depictions match forecasts against mission, system, and platform thresholds, enabling commanders to determine optimal force employment packages in those environmental conditions. Increasingly, decision-makers will interact with the net-centric weather data repository through machine-to-machine interfaces to extract mission-specific information tailored to their needs. Effective tailoring therefore requires that weather forces thoroughly understand how the weather and space environment impacts operations.

INTEGRATE

Effective integration enables decision-makers to maintain battlespace awareness. So armed, they can anticipate the environment's effects on planned operations, then mitigate or exploit those conditions which facilitate achievement of joint force and functional component commanders' objectives. Commanders should ensure environmental effects on operations are fully integrated into decision-making processes and command and control systems.

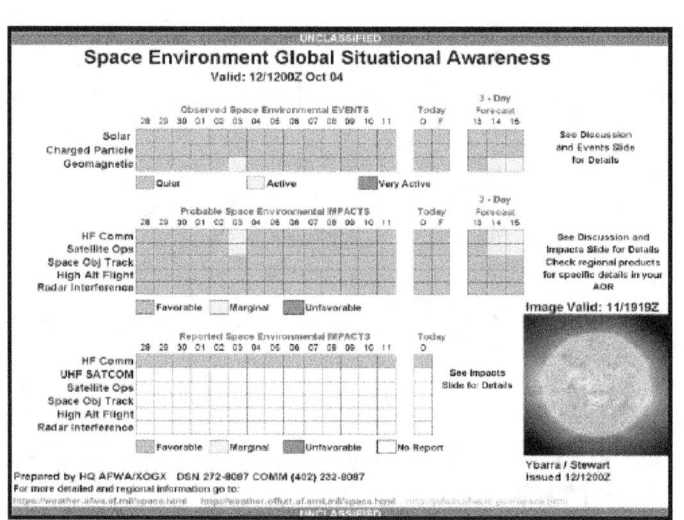

Environmental information should be tailored to unique air, space, and surface operational requirements.

Timeliness is critical to effective integration; therefore, weather operations rely on robust, assured common user communications. Moreover, environmental information is most effective when it is incorporated into command and control systems and processes. A net-centric repository of environmental information and operational impacts facilitates such integration. The net-centric repository also allows individual decision-makers to fuse relevant weather impacts with other operational information into an operational picture tailored to their mission. For example, a pilot would only access weather impacts related to their sortie, whereas a joint force commander would develop depictions of weather impacts to theater-wide operations.

Operation IRAQI FREEDOM
25-27 March 2003

During the American-led march to Baghdad, Air Force weather forces correctly predicted the onset of widespread sandstorms in south-central Iraq 4-5 days in advance. Commanders seized the moment and quickly integrated this environmental information into their operational planning. Scheduled missions were modified or cancelled, and new ones were added. Air Force platforms and weapons systems vulnerable to the expected conditions were switched out in favor of those that could overcome the degrading effects of persistent strong winds that produced blowing sand and near-zero visibilities up to several thousand feet over the area of responsibility. B-52H bombers equipped with satellite-guided joint direct-attack munitions were able to continue attack operations against unsuspecting Republican Guard forces. Once the storms subsided, temporarily disabled US ground troops were able to continue their offensive amidst a weakened Iraqi resistance.

— Various Sources

The integration process requires continuous management. Without effective management, communication paths can become saturated. Collection/communication systems should be designed to deliver environmental information in near-real time.

A familiar example of weather integration for daily operations is the use of weather forecasting and observations in maintaining flightline safety. Working closely with operations and base safety offices, weather support is vital in preventing lightning strikes to personnel, a serious hazard on the large open areas of the flightline. Prevention of weather-related injury to personnel or damage to equipment is a vital role of integrated weather operations. For the warfighter, weather integration would use weather forecasts and observations in targeting. Accurate prediction of winds, clouds and temperature contrasts at or near a target site could influence the selection of approach vectors, time-over-target, and other factors. Integrating weather impacts with intelligence information such as air defense threats allows selection of the safest approaches that maximize lock-on ranges while ensuring the best probability of target kill.

Weather and space effects should be integrated into all facets of operations.

CHAPTER THREE

ORGANIZING, COMMANDING, AND EMPLOYING WEATHER FORCES

> *In Europe bad weather was the worst enemy of the air [operations]. Some soldier once said, "The weather is always neutral." Nothing could be more untrue. Bad weather is obviously the enemy of the side that seeks to launch projects requiring good weather, or of the side possessing great assets, such as strong air forces, which depend upon good weather for effective operations.*
>
> **—General Dwight D. Eisenhower**

GENERAL

The organization of Air Force weather forces is driven by its two distinctly different yet related basic functions: describing past, current and future weather conditions (environmental characterization) and enabling the employment of weather and weather effects information at key decision points (environmental information exploitation). See Figure 3.1 for a comparison of the functions. Due to the extensive processing systems, data storage capacity, and communications capabilities required, environmental characterization is generally accomplished *centrally* from fixed locations employing a high degree of automation. The primary focus is on collection, analysis, and prediction at the *global, regional, and local scales*. Through reachback and/or distributed operations, Air Force weather forces performing this function provide accurate and consistent actionable weather information to those weather forces exploiting environmental information.

COMPARISON OF FEATURES	
Environmental Characterization	**Environmental Information Exploitation**
• Centralized	• Decentralized
• Produce actionable weather information for weather forces	• Produce actionable weather information for decision-makers
• Primarily collect, analyze, and predict	• Primarily tailor and integrate
• Focused on accuracy and consistency	• Focused on relevance and timeliness
• Fixed, large infrastructure	• Mobile, deployable
• Reachback provider	• Reachback user
• Highly automated	• Personal and interactive
• Geographic focus	• Decision-maker focus

Figure 3.1. Comparison of the two functions of Air Force weather operations.

In contrast, *decentralized* weather forces normally support forces conducting operations at the strategic, operational, and tactical levels. Unlike the fixed support associated with environmental characterization, weather forces that exploit environmental information are generally mobile and poised to deploy with supported units. Using the central databases and derived products, these deployable weather forces focus on tailoring and integrating actionable weather information into decision processes at the highest levels of warfare they currently support, whether strategic, operational, or tactical. They also ensure weather information is both timely and relevant, enabling battlespace awareness for supported decision-makers.

ORGANIZING AND COMMANDING WEATHER FORCES

Air Force weather forces organized in units (i.e., squadrons or higher) are normally most effective in producing accurate and consistent past, current, and future representations of the natural environment. Those Air Force weather forces embedded in supported operational units (e.g., a weather flight in an operations support squadron) are most effective at integrating tailored environmental information into operational decision-making processes.

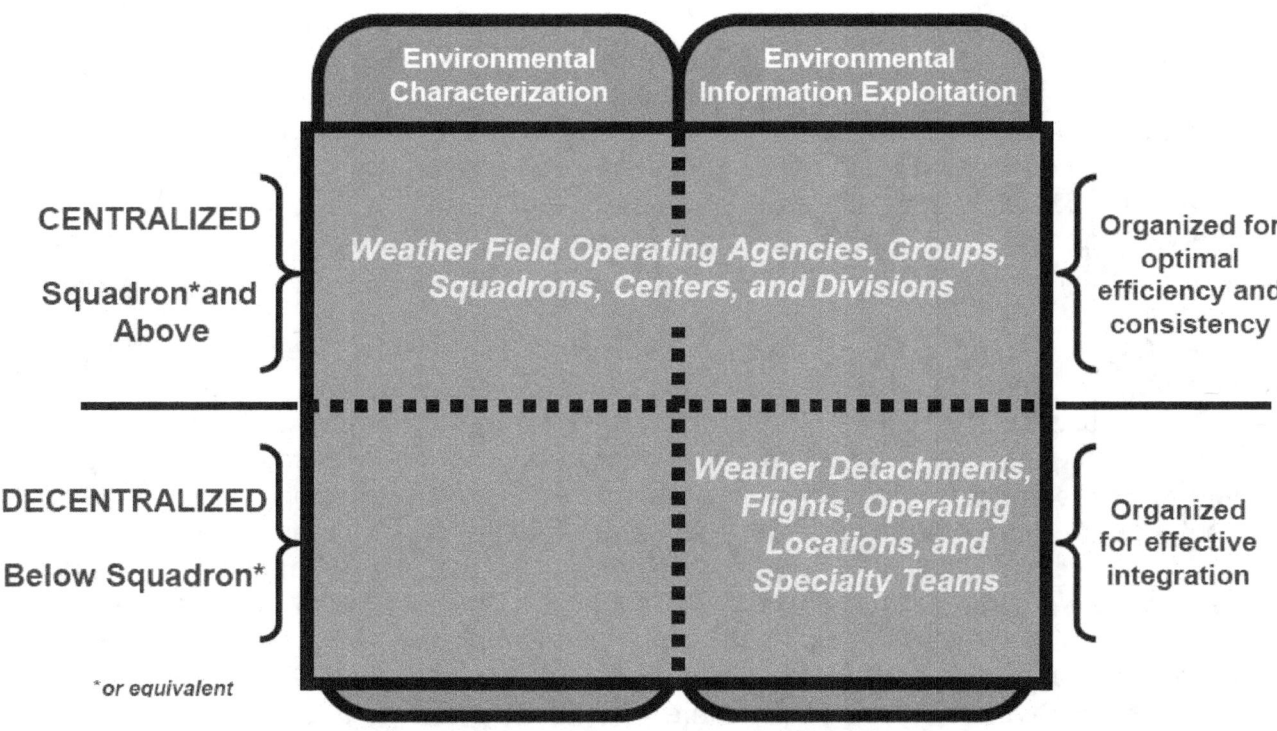

Figure 3.2. Organizing Weather Forces.

Air Force weather forces are normally task-organized to forward deploy with joint force, functional component, and Service component headquarters; air and space operations centers (AOC); Air Force and Army conventional combat units; and Air Force, Army, and joint special operations forces. Air Force weather forces may also

15

contribute to coalition weather operations and may be called upon to assist civil authorities with environmental information. See Figure 3.2 for how weather forces are organized.

Air Force weather operations continuously seek improved efficiency. These efficiencies are typically gained through:

✪ Consolidation of common functions (e.g., airfield forecasting, flight weather services, space launch support, climate/environmental modeling, training).

✪ Consolidation of resources (e.g., force/equipment pools, infrastructure).

✪ Technology (e.g., improved machine-to-machine [M2M] capabilities, common equipment/systems, data fusion).

EMPLOYING WEATHER FORCES

Air Force weather operations with global, regional, and local scopes provide direct support to strategic, operational, and tactical decision-makers through a combination of reachback and distributed operations (e.g., on-site). Air Force weather personnel characterize the environment on global, regional, and local scales, developing information primarily for exploitation by weather forces embedded in operational units. Weather forces directly support decision-makers' requests for assistance at the strategic, operational, and tactical levels to include the national intelligence community; joint force, functional component, and Air Force and Army commanders and staffs; AOCs; expeditionary Air Force units; Army combat arms, combat support, and combat service support; and Air Force and Army special operations units.

Global weather centers collect, compile, process, and format weather and space observations from commercial, civil, and military sources into a four-dimensional representation of the natural environment. They generate computerized real-time analyses, forecasts, long-range outlooks, and climatological assessments of this global natural environment for use at the regional and local levels. Regional weather centers then prepare higher resolution computerized analyses and forecasts, where weather personnel with appropriate regional expertise adjust these outputs to mitigate weaknesses in computer models and algorithms. At the local level, weather personnel collect detailed measurements of the natural environment, which are input into the global database and are the crucial foundation required to develop environmental products suitable for all levels of warfare. Air Force weather operations also process and analyze historical weather data at each level to determine normal seasonal weather patterns, averages, probabilities and effects of specific weather elements on operations. Due to the enormity and complexity of environmental characterization as a whole, Air Force weather operations leverage other DOD and federal capabilities and avoid redundancy whenever practical.

At the base/post level, Air Force weather operations support Air Force air and space units; joint organizations; Army combat, combat support, and combat service support units; and Air Force and Army special operations forces. To do so, weather forces are normally organized as a weather flight in an operations support squadron for Air Force operations or a weather squadron (including subordinate detachments, flights, and operating locations) for Army operations. These weather forces generate specific mission-execution analyses and forecasts for air, space, and surface missions by integrating and tailoring global, regional, and local-scale environmental information with:

✪ Current observations (e.g., surface, solar, and ionospheric conditions, radar, lightning strike data).

✪ Knowledge of friendly and enemy missions, weapons systems, tactics, and environmental sensitivities.

✪ Familiarity with local terrain effects on environmental conditions.

Base/post weather forces contribute to environmental characterization by collecting and disseminating near-real-time weather observations and other local-scale weather data to higher-echelon weather centers. They also provide post-mission feedback on environmental information, such as altitudes and extents of cloud decks, to global and regional weather centers. Air Force weather personnel should be integrated into the warfighting headquarters, AOCs, flying wing/group/squadron mission planning cells and the Army warfighting headquarters military decision-making process (MDMP) to enable warfighters to fully exploit weather and space environmental information. Commanders should also include weather forces in operational exercises (such as RED FLAG, AIR WARRIOR, COPE THUNDER, and Army Battle Command Training Program exercises) to provide combat-related training and experience with aircrews and land operators in simulated, yet realistic, wartime environments.

Since a single weather Airman can support several decision-makers from one location, centralized weather units integrate weather impacts into decision processes where feasible and adequate. This ensures limited human resources are available to embed with operational decision-makers where most critical. For conventional forces, direct support is normally provided down to the Air Force squadron level or the Army brigade combat team/support brigade level. The difference in Air Force and Army operations is mainly driven by the smaller spatial scale of Army brigade-level operations compared to a typical Air Force flying squadron, which may encounter radically different environmental conditions while transiting from the surface through the upper atmosphere over a large area. In contrast, direct support to Army and Air Force special operations forces is normally provided as needed, even to a small, forward-deployed team. Air Force weather operations accomplish direct support through *reachback* (obtaining required information from organizations that are not forward deployed) and through *distributed operations* (conducting weather operations from independent or interdependent nodes through teaming).

Air Force Component Level

The commander, Air Force forces (COMAFFOR)—the air and space expeditionary task force (AETF) commander—exercises operational control (OPCON) of all conventional Air Force weather forces deployed to a theater. Air Force conventional weather personnel generally forward deploy with the combined/joint force air and space component commander (C/JFACC) (if established), AETF subordinate units, and the AOC. See Figure 3.3 for a description of how Air Force weather forces support Air Force and Army forces.

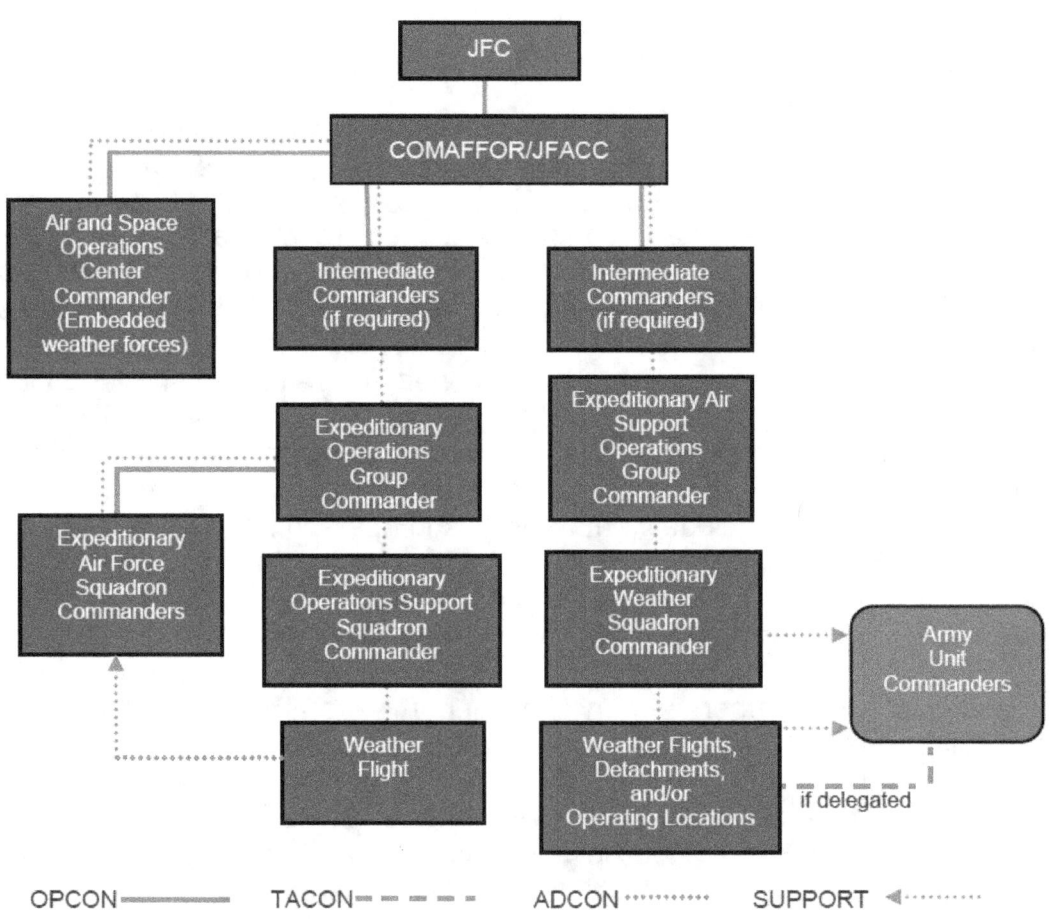

Figure 3.3. Typical command relations for Air Force weather forces supporting conventional Air Force and Army operations.

The combatant commander's supporting Air Force component, usually a major command (MAJCOM) or numbered Air Force (NAF) (the NAF may be superseded by the creation of the warfighting headquarters [WFHQ]), identifies the weather capability needed to support the AETF. In addition, the WFHQ should have weather personnel on the WFHQ A-3 staff and in the AOC. If unable to source the necessary forces, the component forwards requirements for sourcing via the Air and Space Expeditionary

Force Center (AEFC). Whenever possible, Air Force weather forces embedded in operational units should deploy with those units.

The senior Air Force weather representative to the COMAFFOR is designated the COMAFFOR staff weather officer (SWO) and is normally assigned to the A-3 staff. The COMAFFOR SWO monitors Air Force weather operations in theater, including those supporting land forces and SOF, and advises the COMAFFOR A-staff on all matters related to organizing, equipping, training, sustaining, and employing Air Force weather forces. The COMAFFOR SWO should coordinate support responsibilities with the joint meteorological and oceanographic (METOC) officer (JMO), if appointed, or the combatant commander's senior METOC officer (SMO) in accordance with Joint Publication (JP) 3-59, *Joint Doctrine, Tactics, Techniques, and Procedures for Meteorological and Oceanographic Operations*. The COMAFFOR SWO should also coordinate closely with counterparts on other joint force and component staffs, including the chief of the weather specialty team supporting the JFACC's staff. Similar to the COMAFFOR SWO, staff weather officers of other components have functional support responsibilities and should coordinate their respective component requirements directly with the JMO or SMO.

Air and Space Expeditionary Task Force (AETF)

AETFs are task organized to provide required capabilities to meet combatant commander requirements. Based on expected air, space, and surface operational requirements identified by the COMAFFOR in support of JFC objectives, the Air Force component coordinates the task organization of the AETF and arranges for the transfer of forces through the AEFC. Weather personnel should deploy with their supported air expeditionary wing (AEW), group (AEG), squadron (AES), or Army combat unit as part of an AETF. In addition, weather forces from other units, as well as Guard or Reserve personnel, may be tasked to augment AETF weather organizations as part of AEF rotations. Required weather functionality ranges from as few as one Airman or item of tactical meteorological equipment (TACMET) for observations at an unimproved airfield to as much as a contingent of 6-10 Airmen and an accompanying suite of TACMET to conduct 24-hour observing and mission-execution forecasting operations.

Air Force weather forces supporting AEW operations are normally organized, commanded, and employed as a weather flight in an expeditionary operations support squadron (EOSS). As a cross-cutting organization, an EOSS provides flexibility for the deployed weather flight to furnish environmental information to each squadron in the AEW, as well as to AEW support units and the wing operations center. In some instances, it may be best for weather personnel to be directly attached to an AES in order to provide more tailored, specific environmental information in support of AES operations.

Air Force weather forces deployed in an AETF are not self-sufficient. They normally obtain environmental information through reachback and distributed operations from higher-echelon weather organizations, primarily through a supporting operational weather squadron (OWS). **Reachback and distributed operations provide the ability to reliably access environmental information and resources while minimizing the theater footprint.** Deployed weather forces therefore require assured and/or common-user communications to perform their missions.

Air and Space Operations Center (AOC) Weather Operations

The Falconer AOC provides the COMAFFOR with the tools and services required for planning and executing operations with air and space forces. Air Force weather forces are normally organized as a weather specialty team (WST), a horizontally cross-cutting capability integrated into the five AOC divisions (Figure 3.4). The WST also supports other specialty teams such as the battlefield coordination detachment and the joint personnel recovery center. The WST size and internal structure should be inherently flexible and responsive to the changing requirements of the operation. The senior weather officer assigned to the AOC leads the WST and ensures team members are used effectively throughout the AOC. WST personnel should be fully qualified at the AOC field training unit before being assigned to an AOC.

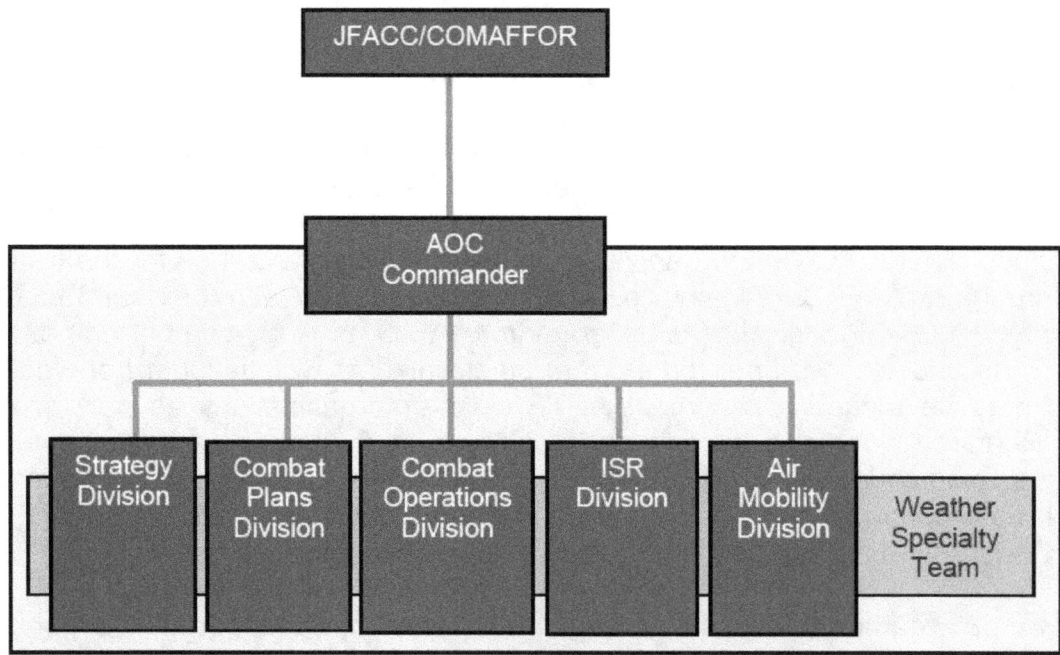

Figure 3.4. The WST is a horizontally cross-cutting capability supporting all AOC divisions.

The WST normally reaches back to centralized weather centers (generally a supporting OWS) for a significant portion of environmental information needed to support AOC operations. The WST therefore requires immediate and sustained connectivity (both secure and nonsecure) to base networks for steady receipt of environmental data. Air Force Operational Tactics, Techniques, and Procedures (AFOTTP) 2-3.2, *Air and Space Operations Center*, contains detailed guidance on employing Air Force weather forces in the AOC.

Functional AOCs also employ weather operations as a force multiplier. In the space AOC, weather forces are normally embedded within the combat operations division's space situational awareness (SSA) team. SSA weather forces should leverage Air Force Weather Agency (AFWA) space weather branch capabilities to identify space weather impacts to terrestrial and space systems, anomalies, assessments and forecasts for all space AOC operations. AFOTTP 2-3.4, *Space Air and Space Operations Center*,

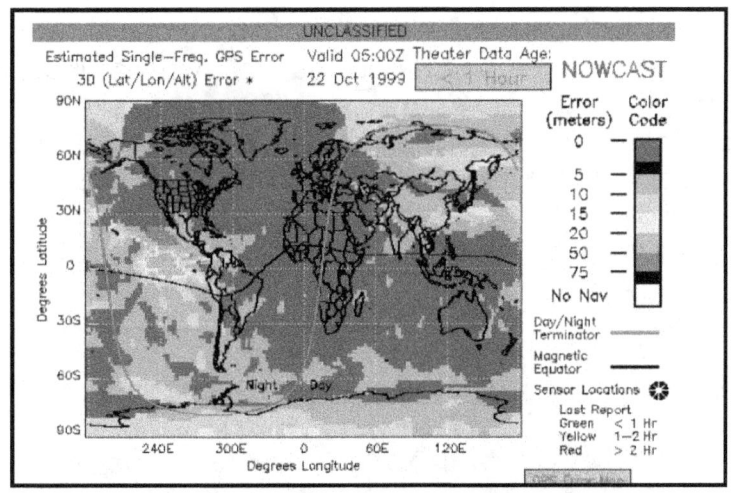

The Space Weather Branch supports Air Force space force employment.

contains a detailed description of Air Force weather operations in the space AOC.

Weather operations in the tanker airlift control center (TACC), another functional AOC, directly support the global air mobility mission of Air Mobility Command. TACC weather forces provide direct mission planning/ execution products and services for the TACC and strategic airlift and tanker crews operating worldwide. Through reachback, TACC weather forces also support deployed elements of contingency response groups as needed. AFOTTP 2-3.5, *Global Mobility Air and Space Operations Center*, contains a detailed description of Air Force weather operations in the TACC.

Joint and Multinational Operations

Air Force weather capabilities should be integrated with those of other Services and nations to provide coherent and structured weather operations to joint and multinational forces. To this end, Air Force weather personnel should be tasked to fill some joint weather positions on a JFC, JFACC, or joint force land component commander (JFLCC) staff or within a joint/combined air and space operations center (J/CAOC). For instance, an Air Force weather officer generally serves as either the SMO or the JMO. In particular, for air and space- or land-centric operations in which the Air Force or Army provides the preponderance of forces, an Air Force field grade weather officer should be appointed as the JMO. When a joint task force is formed, Air Force weather forces may also be tasked to form or augment a joint METOC forecast unit (JMFU). Alternatively, an existing Air Force METOC organization, such as an OWS, may be established as a JMFU. Roles, responsibilities, organizations, and principles of joint weather operations are further discussed in JP 3-59, *Joint Doctrine, Tactics, Techniques, and Procedures for Meteorological and Oceanographic Operations*.

Special Operations Forces (SOF)

Air Force weather forces also provide direct environmental support to the unique worldwide missions of special operations forces. To do so, Air Force weather operations must field technically and tactically skilled, fully mission-qualified weather forces ready to deploy worldwide on short notice. In addition, SOF weather forces must be capable of infiltrating the joint operations area via sea, air, and land and of operating independently in permissive and uncertain environments and with other SOF teams in hostile areas.

Operation EAGLE CLAW: A Hard Lesson to Learn

 *Top-secret planning for what would be one of the most complicated and ambitious raids in American history, the Iranian hostage rescue attempt of 1980, lasted well over five months but it fell short of fully considering an incorrigible foe: the weather.*

Historical records pointed to winter as the optimal time for a mission of this type, as limited moonlight and suitable temperatures and densities represented favorable conditions for night RH-53D operations. Nevertheless, the mission was set for late April, introducing additional weather challenges such as suspended dust, which proved to be a factor in the subsequent mishap. This mission-impacting information was never briefed to JTF planners and decision-makers....

Recommendations to use a WC-130 weather reconnaissance aircraft as a scout in advance of the RH-53Ds were discounted based on assumed favorable weather conditions and for security reasons. Additionally, it was determined that pilot reports from accompanying C-130s, flying the same route, could provide advance notice of unfavorable weather as needed. However, the C-130s ended up arriving at the destination, Desert One, well ahead of the helicopters and were unable to relay up-to-the-minute weather data to the RH-53D crews.

Weather operations personnel were excluded from planning and rehearsal exercises at the JTF training areas, eliminating their ability to work with the aircrews..... Furthermore, mission execution weather briefings, developed by weather operations personnel, were presented by J-2 intelligence officers who had little, if any, formal weather training or experience. Aircrew feedback was provided in the same indirect way. Pilots were thus unaware of the possibility of encountering suspended dust and were unprepared to handle it. Integration of weather information, a vital contributor to mission success, never occurred.

—**Paul B. Ryan**
The Iranian Rescue Mission: Why It Failed

The lack of weather preparations in Operation EAGLE CLAW cost the United States military equipment, effectiveness, and, most importantly, lives.

If a joint special operations task force (JSOTF) is established, the joint force special operations component commander (JFSOCC), in coordination with a designated JFSOCC SWO, determines the correct mix of SOF weather forces required to support JFC objectives. Normally, SOF perform best when weather forces are embedded in the deploying SOF team. The SOF team's weather component is tailored appropriately for a given scenario.

SOF operate in the forward and deep battlespace, areas in which METOC data are often sparse or denied. Embedded SOF weather forces, therefore, offer a capability to obtain forward-area METOC observations in support of conventional and SOF missions. Furthermore, this vital information should be quickly disseminated to centralized weather organizations where it can be exploited to enhance the accuracy of global and regional analyses and forecasts. SOF weather forces leverage centrally produced environmental characterization information through a combination of reachback and distributed operations to generate tailored environmental impact information for specific SOF missions. SOF weather forces also train and liaise with indigenous persons.

Conventional US Army Operations

By inter-Service agreement initiated as a result of the National Security Act of 1947, Air Force weather operations support Army air and ground combat arms, combat support, and combat service support units. Weather and weather impact information are integral to the MDMP, including intelligence preparation of the battlespace, and contribute to dominant battlespace awareness, enabling the Army to achieve information and decision superiority. Since the natural environment affects friendly as well as hostile forces, Air Force weather operations should fully understand the environmental sensitivities of friendly and enemy land force capabilities.

To become more relevant to combatant commanders, the Army is transforming into a force of modular, self-contained, lethal force packages organized with capabilities to accomplish the full range of missions, i.e., from major combat to stability operations. To support such a force, Air Force weather operations must be flexible, responsive, and tailorable.

Weather squadrons supporting Army operations should be habitually aligned with designated Army combat and combat support units. When appropriate, the squadron commander tailors a weather force to forward deploy in support of any combination of these designated units. To do so, Air Force weather operations must field technically and tactically skilled weather forces ready to deploy worldwide and be capable of operating with Army forces in permissive, uncertain, and hostile operating environments. To be consistent with JP 3-59, weather forces supporting operations should be integrated through the G-3 (operations) and support the G-2 (intelligence) and other decision-makers as required. The supporting weather squadron should provide appropriate weather representation on the commander, Army forces' G-3 staff to assist the COMAFFOR SWO in organizing, training, equipping, sustaining, and employing Air Force weather forces supporting Army operations.

Forward-deployed Air Force weather forces supporting Army operations leverage environmental characterization information from centralized weather organizations via a combination of reachback and distributed operations to provide tailored environmental effects information essential to planning and executing land operations. To do so, weather forces supporting Army operations require robust, assured common-user communications. Air Force weather operations should be seamlessly integrated with Army command and control systems and processes at all echelons. Machine-to-machine interfaces enhance such integration.

FIXED US AIR FORCE WEATHER OPERATIONS

Fixed, centralized weather units generally perform the environmental characterization function of Air Force weather operations, particularly at the global and regional scales. Deployed Air Force weather forces and personnel are best supported by these in-place capabilities primarily via reachback and distributed operations. Other non-deployable organizations directly support decision-makers conducting air, space, and surface missions at the tactical, operational, or strategic levels. In some cases, both functions of Air Force weather operations are conducted within a single agency. Key fixed Air Force weather organizations are described below.

Air Force Weather Agency. The Air Force Weather Agency (AFWA), a field operating agency reporting to the Director of Weather, Headquarters USAF, includes the primary production center for Air Force weather operations. AFWA collects and processes worldwide atmospheric and space data, develops global-scale analyses and forecasts, runs prediction models, and produces and disseminates a variety of environmental information. In addition, AFWA possesses a just-in-time capability to

---

DESERT STORM: Space Enters the Fray

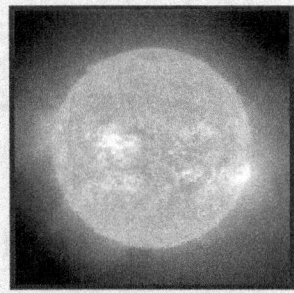

Operation DESERT STORM featured an expanded use of weather, navigation, early warning, and surveillance satellites, compelling warfighters to consider the space environment's impacts on their operations. DESERT STORM not only occurred during the height of the third largest solar maximum on record, but it was also conducted in an overall significantly hostile natural environment. During the 41-day war, 81 major solar flares occurred.

These flares degraded performance of communication systems for minutes to hours and impacted other satellite systems as well. In addition to sporadic disturbances like solar flares, the daily variation in the ionosphere over equatorial regions created scintillation problems on Southwest Asian satellite and UHF communications during the evening hours. Commanders should be aware of space environmental effects on potential operations during planning and COA development.

—Various Sources

focus technical expertise and computer-intensive forecast models on particular theaters of interest to meet operational requirements. AFWA also submits requirements for on-board sensor tasking of Defense Meteorological Satellite Program satellites in support of specific DOD and national-level operations.

AFWA monitors solar activity (such as sunspots, solar flares, or coronal mass ejections) and solar wind characteristics (such as energetic particles, shock waves, or magnetic fields) at numerous surveillance sites around the globe and from space. AFWA's space weather branch, the sole DOD organization providing mission-tailored analyses and forecasts of system-impacting space weather, uses these data to generate worldwide warnings of operationally significant space environmental activity.

AFWA's intelligence community (IC) weather branch provides planning and execution space and terrestrial weather analyses, forecasts, climate assessments, and mission-tailored decision aids at the highest levels of security for multibillion dollar IC operations, including those of the National Reconnaissance Office (NRO), National Security Agency (NSA), Central Intelligence Agency (CIA), National Geospatial-Intelligence Agency (NGA), and other IC agencies.

AFWA's special operations support branch supports worldwide SOF operations, even down to the individual team level, through secure reachback. The branch also provides tailored meteorological information for end-to-end planning at US Special Operations Command (USSOCOM), Service component special operations commands, and theater special operations commands.

AFWA's meteorological satellite (METSAT) applications branch produces rapid response, tailored METSAT imagery and evaluation for DOD contingency operations and generates automated METSAT imagery products for web-based distribution to DOD users. The branch is also the DOD focal point for global volcanic ash event monitoring, advisories, and trajectory forecasts.

Air Force Combat Climatology Center (AFCCC). Climatological data, the typical weather conditions for a given location or region, provide valuable first-look environmental information for decision making such as course of action selection (should the offensive begin before winter?) and logistics planning (are heaters or air conditioners needed? Snow removal equipment or bulldozers?). To meet this need, AFCCC processes and analyzes historical weather data to determine normal seasonal patterns, averages and probabilities for the entire world. AFCCC can also provide tailored

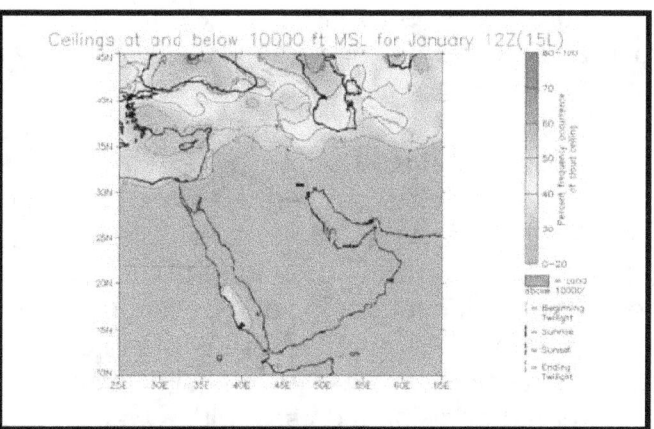

Climatological data from AFCCC can greatly assist air and space power decision makers and planners.

operational climatologies for various mission profiles based on specific weather threshold sensitivities.

AFCCC plays a key role as the modeling and simulation (M&S) executive agent for the air and space natural environment, injecting weather into DOD, joint, and Service war games and simulations. AFCCC can also create modeled climatological information for data-sparse regions, offering an initial estimate of expected conditions in an area where actual historical information is unavailable.

Joint Typhoon Warning Center (JTWC). The JTWC, comprised of Air Force weather and Navy METOC personnel, provides tropical cyclone forecasts and warnings for DOD, Department of State, and other US government assets in the Pacific and Indian Oceans.

Operational Weather Squadrons (OWS). The OWS is the Air Force's primary regionally focused weather unit. Whether in peace or at war, OWS provide multiple-scale environmental information and serve as centers of regional weather expertise in support of a combatant commander's air, space, and surface operations. OWS develop analyses, forecasts, and weather effects information for command and control activities as well as deployed weather forces. Products include but are not limited to theater-wide weather; drop zone/range/air refueling forecasts/flight managed mission support; fine-scale target forecasts; airfield forecasts; and watches, warnings, and advisories for fixed or deployed Air Force and Army locations within their assigned areas. An OWS is also a source of dedicated environmental information for command and control processes at AOCs. When warfighting units do not have assigned weather forces, the supporting OWS should fulfill this role as capabilities permit.

During joint operations, a combatant commander, through the SMO or JMO, may designate an OWS as the JMFU in accordance with JP 3-59. When established as the JMFU, an OWS is responsible for the joint operational area forecast (JOAF), the official planning forecast for all components of the joint force. In addition, as a JMFU the OWS monitors the effectiveness of the theater collection plan in meeting the needs of the overall operation. For extended operations, an OWS designated as the JMFU normally requires augmentation.

Staff Meteorologists (StaffMets). Advanced-degree research, acquisition, and test meteorologists support Air Force Materiel Command at various locations. These StaffMets perform or support basic research as well as the development, acquisition, and testing of Air Force weapons, weapons systems, and other capabilities by identifying, documenting, and resolving environmental sensitivity issues and weather information requirements. StaffMets interface with program managers to identify critical weapons system weather sensitivities/thresholds. A key source of such data for automated decision aids as well as weather forces exploiting environmental information, StaffMets are also employed within the intelligence and space communities to perform similar technical consultation services for weather-sensitive systems under development or conducting operations.

CHAPTER FOUR

TRAINING AND EDUCATION

We can't change the weather, but we can change our operations to conform to the weather.

—General Henry H. "Hap" Arnold

GENERAL

Successful air, space, and surface operations rely in part on the effective training and education of all Airmen and Soldiers on the potential impacts of the natural environment to friendly and enemy capabilities across the range of military operations. Decision-makers should further understand the capabilities and limitations of weather operations and be trained to exploit weather information at every decision point throughout the planning, execution, assessment, and sustainment of military operations. To meet this objective, Air Force weather personnel should fully understand the natural environment, apply that knowledge to ascertain potential environmental effects on military operations, and integrate that assessment into decision processes anywhere, anytime. Consequently, **Air Force weather operations employ Airmen educated in the sciences of meteorology and space physics, trained to couple this science with the art of warfare, and capable of operating in permissive, uncertain, and hostile environments.**

Non-weather Personnel

All Airmen should understand that weather can adversely impact friendly and enemy operations, and that it may do so asymmetrically, possibly offering friendly forces an exploitable advantage. Accordingly, knowledge of weather conditions and the potential impacts on weapons systems, tactics, timelines, and other parameters is necessary for effective decision-making. Weather information, exploited at every decision point during the planning, execution, assessment, and sustainment of military operations at every level of war, is a key enabler of air and space power functions.

Non-weather personnel, particularly commanders, staffs, mission planners, logisticians, and other decision-makers should be aware of and, where appropriate, trained on how to not only identify the impacts of weather on air, space, and surface operations, but also how to use weather information to their strategic, operational, or tactical advantage. This training should be provided in a variety of Service and joint venues, to include commander's preparatory courses, weapons school classes, AOC courses, exercises, wargames, seminars, and simulations.

Every Airman should participate in challenging training fora, including exercises and war games, in which realistic environmental conditions impact the mission capability of friendly and enemy forces. Moreover, these fora should reward decision- makers for smartly exploiting weather information while penalizing those who neglect to consider weather impacts. To achieve these objectives, Air Force weather forces should maintain a robust environmental modeling and simulation capability that can be easily integrated into exercises, war games, and other appropriate venues.

Weather Personnel

Formal education and training encompassing weather and space physics, operational art, and field skills are continuing processes throughout an individual's career, progressing through the basic, intermediate, and advanced levels. Although all Air Force weather personnel possess a blend of these capabilities, the education and training emphasis on a given skill set is highly mission dependent. Nominal examples are depicted in Figure 4.1.

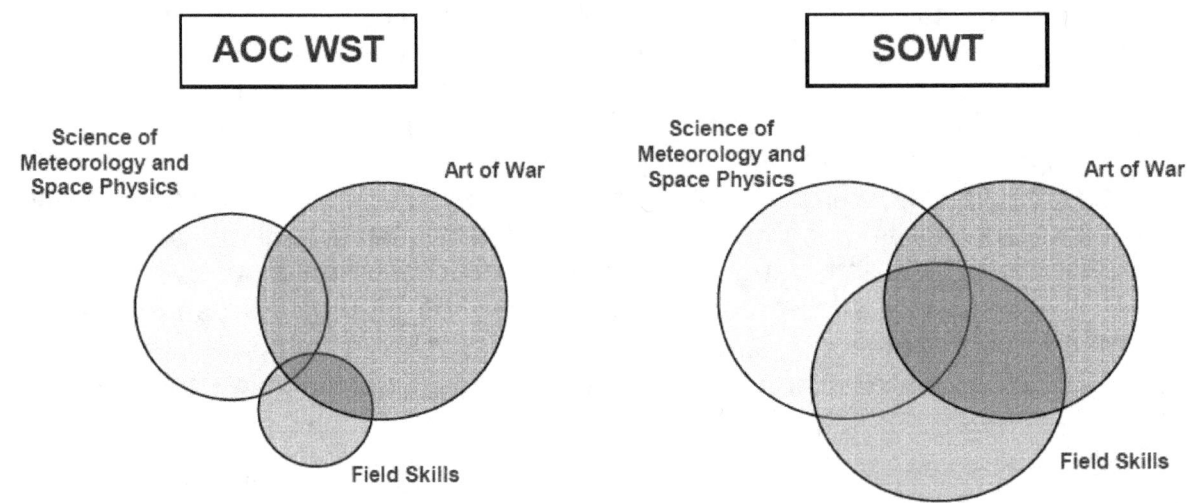

Figure 4.1. Nominal required skill sets for personnel assigned to an AOC weather specialty team (AOC WST) or a special operations weather team (SOWT). The size of the circle is proportional to the emphasis on the identified skill.

Weather personnel should receive technical education and training through a blend of classroom, laboratory, and on-the-job training, built on the foundation of a formalized initial skills course and solidified via upgrade/duty qualification training. Additionally, commanders and functional managers should ensure weather personnel receive tailored continuation and advanced technical training necessary to perform specific individual duties at the unit level.

In addition to maintaining great depth in understanding scientific parameters and technical processes, Air Force weather personnel should also know how the environment and environmental information contribute to the success of military operations. Continuous education and training on the art of war, air and space power, joint force employment, and the exploitation of weather information for operational purposes ensure Air Force weather forces understand how properly integrated weather information can act as a force multiplier for decision-makers. Developmental education, coupled with developmental and joint assignments, contribute to this broader knowledge of air, space, and surface operations.

All Air Force personnel should meet and maintain minimum Air Force personal readiness standards, such as weapons proficiency, in order to operate in bare-base locations anywhere in the world. In addition, Air Force weather personnel are often employed with SOF and conventional Army forces in uncertain and hostile environments well outside the airbase perimeter. These Battlefield Airmen should therefore be further trained individually and collectively to shoot, move, and communicate in the modern battlespace. Weather forces that deploy with special operations forces should also maintain a capability to infiltrate the area of operations via air, land, or sea.

In addition to classroom, laboratory, computer/web-based, and on-the-job training, Air Force weather forces should regularly participate in realistic Service and joint exercises, war games, and other venues to achieve and maintain proficiency and readiness. Realistic exercises identify possible shortfalls and help determine corrective actions necessary to achieve success in future operations. Exercises should focus on the skills and tools needed by individuals and units conducting weather operations and can help ensure staffs are able to plan, control, and support these operations. Furthermore, several resources exist to educate the Airman in weather operations. Tactics, techniques, and procedures are increasingly emphasizing weather in tactical operations and are an excellent resource for the warfighter.

At the very heart of warfare lies doctrine...

Suggested Readings

Air Force Publications   (Note: All Air Force doctrine documents are available on the Air Force Doctrine Center web page at **https://www.doctrine.af.mil**)

AFDD 1, *Air Force Basic Doctrine*

AFDD 2, *Organization and Employment*

AFDD 2-1, *Air Warfare*

AFDD 2-2, *Space Operations*

AFDD 2-4, *Combat Support*

AFDD 2-6, *Air Mobility Operations*

AFDD 2-7, *Special Operations*

AFDD 2-8, *Command and Control*

AFDD 2-9, *Intelligence, Surveillance, and Reconnaissance Operations*

Air Force Policy Directive 15-1, *Atmospheric and Space Environmental Support*

Air Force Instruction 15-128, *Air and Space Weather Operations – Roles and Responsibilities*

Air Force Manual (AFMAN) 15-129, *Air and Space Weather Operations – Processes and Procedures*

Air Force Space Command Pamphlet 15-2, *Space Environmental Impacts on DOD Operations*

Air Force Weather Strategic Plan and Vision FY2008-2032, January 2004

Air Force Operational Tactics, Techniques, and Procedures (AFOTTP) 2-3.2, *Air and Space Operations Center*

Air Force Operational Tactics, Techniques, and Procedures (AFOTTP) 2-3.4, *Space Air and Space Operations Center*

Air Force Operational Tactics, Techniques, and Procedures (AFOTTP) 2-3.5, *Global Mobility Air and Space Operations Center*

Air Force Tactics, Techniques, and Procedures (AFTTP) 3-1 series

Joint Publications (JPs)

JP 0-2, *Unified Action Armed Forces*

JP 1-02, *Department of Defense Dictionary of Military and Associated Terms*

JP 3-30, *Command and Control for Joint Air Operations*

JP 3-59, *Joint Doctrine, Tactics, Techniques, and Procedures for Meteorological and Oceanographic Operations*

Joint METOC Handbook

Chairman of the Joint Chiefs of Staff Instruction 3810.01B, *Meteorological and Oceanographic Operations*

Other Service Publications

Joint Army Regulation 115-10/Air Force Joint Instruction 15-157, *Weather Support for the US Army*

Field Manual 34-81/AFMAN 105-4, *Weather Support for Army Tactical Operations*

Allied Joint Pub 3.11, *Allied Doctrine for METOC Support to Joint Forces*

Other Publications

Arnold, H.H., *Global Mission.* Harper & Brothers, 1949.

Bates, Charles C. and Fuller, John F., *America's Weather Warriors: 1814-1985*, Texas A&M University Press, 1986.

Brown, Harvey E., *The Medical Department of the United States Army from 1775 to 1875.* Washington Surgeon General's Office, 1973.

Eisenhower, Dwight D., *Crusade in Europe.* Doubleday & Co., 1948.

Fuller, John F., *Weather and War.* Office of MAC History, 1974.

Fuller, John F., *Thor's Legions: Weather Support to the US Air Force and Army, 1937-1987.* American Meteorological Society Historical Monograph, 1990.

Lanicci, John M., "Integrating Weather Exploitation into Airpower and Space Power Doctrine", Airpower Journal 12, No. 2 (Summer 1998), 52-63.

Lanicci, John M., "Weather Operations in the Transformation Era", Air War College Maxwell Paper No. 29, Air University Press, March 2003.

Winters, Harold A., *Battling the Elements: Weather and Terrain in the Conduct of War,* Johns Hopkins University Press, 1998.

GLOSSARY

Abbreviations and Acronyms

ACC	Air Combat Command
AEFC	Air and Space Expeditionary Force Center
AES	air expeditionary squadron
AETF	air and space expeditionary task force
AEW	air expeditionary wing
AFCCC	Air Force Combat Climatology Center
AFDC	Air Force Doctrine Center
AFDD	Air Force doctrine document
AMC	Air Mobility Command
AFWA	Air Force Weather Agency
AOC	air and space operations center
AOR	area of responsibility
CJTF	commander, joint task force
COA	course of action
COD	combat operations division
COMAFFOR	commander, Air Force forces
CSAR	combat search and rescue
DIRMOBFOR-AIR	director of air mobility forces
EOSS	expeditionary operations support squadron
GPS	global positioning system
ISR	intelligence, surveillance, and reconnaissance
JFACC	joint force air and space component commander
JFC	joint force commander
JFLCC	joint force land component commander
JFSOCC	joint force special operations component commander
JMFU	joint meteorological and oceanographic forecast unit
JOAF	joint operational area forecast
JTF	joint task force
JMO	Joint METOC Officer
METOC	meteorological and oceanographic
METSAT	meteorological satellite
NAF	numbered Air Force
OWS	operational weather squadron

PBA	predictive battlespace awareness
PIREPS	pilot reports
SA	situational awareness
SATCOM	satellite communications
SMO	senior meteorological and oceanographic officer
SOF	special operations forces
SOWT	special operation weather team
SWO	staff weather officer
TACC	tanker airlift control center
TACS	theater air control system
TACMET	tactical meteorological equipment
TET	targeting and effects translation
TST	time-sensitive target
UHF	ultra high frequency
US	United States
WST	weather specialty team

Definitions

air and space expeditionary task force. A deployed numbered Air Force (NAF) or command echelon immediately subordinate to a NAF provided as the US Air Force component command committed to a joint operation. Also called **AETF.** (JP 1-02) [*The organizational manifestation of Air Force forces afield. The AETF provides a joint force commander with a task-organized, integrated package with the appropriate balance of force, sustainment, control, and force protection.*] (AFDD 1) {Italicized words in brackets apply only to the Air Force and are offered for clarity.}

air and space power. The synergistic application of air, space, and information systems to project global strategic military power. (AFDD 1)

Battlefield Airmen (BA). BA directly assist, control, enable, and/or execute operational air and space power functions in the forward battlespace independent of an established airbase or its perimeter defenses. Comprising several Air Force Specialties, BA primarily operate as surface combatants removed from traditional airbase support, logistics, and sortie generation efforts. (AFPD 10-35)

battlespace awareness. The environment, factors, and conditions that must be understood to successfully apply combat power, protect the force, or complete the mission. This includes air, land, sea, space, and the included enemy and friendly forces; facilities; weather; terrain; the electronic spectrum; and the information environment within the operational areas and areas of interest. (JP 1-02).

direct support. A mission requiring a force to support another specific force and authorizing it to answer directly to the supported force's request for assistance. (JP 1-02).

distributed operations. The process of conducting operations from independent or interdependent nodes in a teaming manner. Some operational planning or decision-making may occur from outside the joint area of operations. The goal of a distributed operation is to support the operational commander in the field; it is not a method of command from the rear. (AFDD 2-8).

global positioning system. A satellite constellation that provides highly accurate position, velocity, and time navigation information to users. Also called **GPS.** (JP 1-02)

intelligence, surveillance, and reconnaissance. Integrated capabilities to collect, process, exploit and disseminate accurate and timely information that provides the battlespace awareness necessary to successfully plan and conduct operations. (AFDD 2-5.2)

joint. Connotes activities, operations, organizations, etc., in which elements of two or more military departments participate. (JP 1–02)

joint force air component commander. The commander within a unified command, subordinate unified command, or joint task force responsible to the establishing commander for making recommendations on the proper employment of assigned, attached, and/or made available for tasking air forces; planning and coordinating air operations; or accomplishing such operational missions as may be assigned. The joint force air component commander is given the authority necessary to accomplish missions and tasks assigned by the establishing commander. Also called **JFACC.** (JP 1-02) [*The joint force air and space component commander uses the joint air and space operations center to command and control the integrated air and space effort to meet joint force commander's objectives. The Air Force position is that air power and space power together create effects that cannot be achieved through air or space power alone.*] (AFDD 2) {Italicized words in brackets apply only to the Air Force and are offered for clarity.}

joint force commander. A general term applied to a combatant commander, subunified commander, or joint task force commander authorized to exercise combatant command (command authority) or operational control over a joint force. Also called **JFC.** (JP 1–02)

joint force special operations component commander. The commander within a unified command, subordinate unified command, or joint task force responsible to the establishing commander for making recommendations on the proper employment of assigned, attached, and/or made available for tasking special operations forces and assets; planning and coordinating special operations; or accomplishing such operational missions as may be assigned. The joint force special operations component commander is given the authority necessary to accomplish missions and tasks assigned by the establishing commander. Also called **JFSOCC**. (JP 1-02)

operational level of war. The level of war at which campaigns and major operations are planned, conducted, and sustained to accomplish strategic objectives within theaters or other operational areas. Activities at this level link tactics and strategy by establishing operational objectives needed to accomplish the strategic objectives, sequencing events to achieve the operational objectives, initiating actions, and applying resources to bring about and sustain these events. These activities imply a broader dimension of time or space than do tactics; they ensure the logistic and administrative support of tactical forces, and provide the means by which tactical successes are exploited to achieve strategic objectives. See also **strategic level of war; tactical level of war.** (JP 1-02)

reachback. The process of obtaining products, services, and applications, or forces, or equipment, or material from organizations that are not forward deployed. (JP 1-02)

strategic level of war. The level of war at which a nation, often as a member of a group of nations, determines national or multinational (alliance or coalition) security objectives and guidance, and develops and uses national resources to accomplish these objectives. Activities at this level establish national and multinational military objectives; sequence initiatives; define limits and assess risks for the use of military and other instruments of national power; develop global plans or theater war plans to achieve these objectives; and provide military forces and other capabilities in accordance with strategic plans. See also **operational level of war; tactical level of war.** (JP 1-02)

special operations forces. Those active and Reserve component forces of the military Services designated by the Secretary of Defense and specifically organized, trained, and equipped to conduct and support special operations. Also called **SOF**. (JP 1-02)

special operations weather team. A task-organized team of Air Force personnel organized, trained, and equipped to collect critical weather observations from data-sparse areas. These teams are trained to operate independently in permissive or uncertain environments, or as augmentation to other special operations elements in hostile environments, in direct support of special operations. Also called **SOWT**. (AFDD 2-9.1)

tactical level of war. The level of war at which battles and engagements are planned and executed to accomplish military objectives assigned to tactical units or task forces. Activities at this level focus on the ordered arrangement and maneuver of combat elements in relation to each other and to the enemy to achieve combat objectives. See also **operational level of war; strategic level of war.** (JP 1-02)